A DAY AT THE RACES

A DAY AT THE RACES

WRITTEN AND PHOTOGRAPHED BY HAROLD ROTH

Pantheon Books / NEW YORK

For Tommy and Mike
my original racing buddies

I would like to thank the following for their
invaluable assistance: Frank Wright; David Wyland;
Almer Huntley, Jr.; Nick Gonzales; Raymond Haight;
Elaine Brandon; Horace (Blue) Rappelyea; and all
the early-rising, hardworking horse lovers who
appear in this book.
  I would also like to thank Beth Seinfeld for inspiration;
Denise Cronin, Monica Klein, Colleen Brennan, and
Laura Woodworth for support; and Dinah Stevenson,
my editor, for keeping me on track.

Library of Congress Cataloging in Publication Data
Roth, Harold.   A day at the races.
Summary: Describes the activities of a typical day
at the racetrack, including the work of the
trainers, grooms, hot walkers, exercise riders,
blacksmiths, and veterinarians.
1. Horse-racing—Juvenile literature.
[1. Horse racing] I. Title.
SF335.6.R67 1983   798.4'3   83-2345
ISBN 0-394-85814-X
ISBN 0-394-95814-4 (lib. bdg.)

A THOROUGHBRED racehorse in action is as thrilling a sight as you'll ever see. The speed, suspense, and drama of racing pull thousands of cheering fans to their feet at every racetrack every day. The horses seem to share the excitement of the spectators as they concentrate all their strength and energy on reaching their goal: to be first across the finish line.

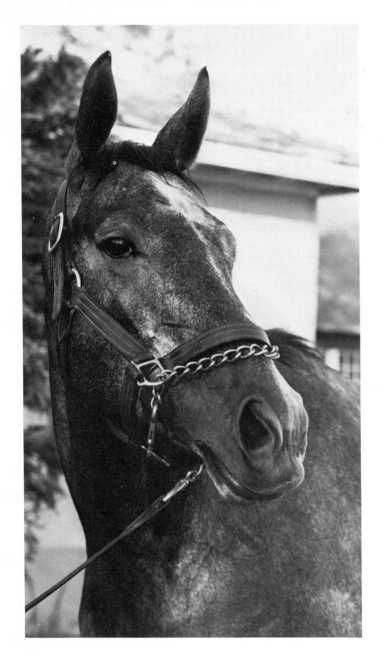

The Thoroughbred is no ordinary horse. Among the fastest animals in the world, Thoroughbreds are bred specifically for racing. For over two hundred years horsemen have been breeding these racehorses, which excel not only in speed but also in stamina and "heart"—a combination of gameness and courage that means the horse will give its best at all times.

It takes more than breeding to make a champion. Thoroughbred racehorses are highly trained athletes. It takes a lot of dedicated people, working together as a team, to bring them to the races in top condition. These people include trainers, grooms, hot walkers, exercise riders, blacksmiths, and veterinarians.

When you think about a racetrack, you probably picture the part where the horses run. But there's more to the track than the racing oval. Far from the grandstand is the area known as the backside of the racetrack. During the racing season this is where the horses live, eat, sleep, and train for the races. There are stables and training facilities for the horses, lots of trees, and plenty of room for the horses to walk around.

The day's activity begins here, before the sun rises.

The first sound of the day is horses neighing and pawing the ground as they wait for their morning feeding. The horses live in wooden stalls about ten feet square. The floor of the stalls is covered with a thick layer of straw and hay. The "hay bed" is absorbent, and it is more comfortable for a horse to stand on than the hard floor would be.

The groom is the first of the stable hands to arrive, usually at about 4:30 A.M. A groom is hired by a trainer to take care of three or four of the horses that are the trainer's responsibility. The groom gives those horses food and water, cleans out their stalls, washes them down, bandages their legs, takes them to and from the races, and generally cares for their appearance.

Grooms spend a lot of time with the horses, and a special relationship develops between them.

A horse in training eats between six and ten quarts of oats and grain, as well as up to twenty-five pounds of hay or grass, each day, and drinks gallons and gallons of water.

The groom gives the horses fresh water, puts hay in the hayracks, and prepares the morning feed, mixing vitamins and other supplements with the oats and grain. Horses that are finicky eaters may have a sweetener, molasses or honey, added to their feed.

Between 5:30 and 6:00 the rest of the stable hands, and the trainer, arrive for work. The trainer is hired by the owner of the horses to see that the horses are in the best possible condition for racing. The trainer is in charge of, and responsible for, everything that goes on in the stable: hiring and supervising stable hands, scheduling visits by the blacksmith and veterinarian, planning every horse's exercise and diet, deciding what races the horses should be entered in, choosing and instructing the jockeys who will ride them.

Most trainers post a training schedule each day to let the stable hands know what needs to be done. Each horse is identified by name and stall number, and the type of workout is specified: the gait (G for gallop or W for walk), or a particular distance.

While they are in their stalls, horses wear bandages around their legs. Horses tend to develop nervous habits like kicking the sides of the stall. The bandages help protect their ankles and legs from injury.

By 6:00 or 6:30 the horses have had a chance to digest their breakfast and relax for a while and are ready for their daily exercise. The groom removes the protective bandages before taking a horse out of the stall.

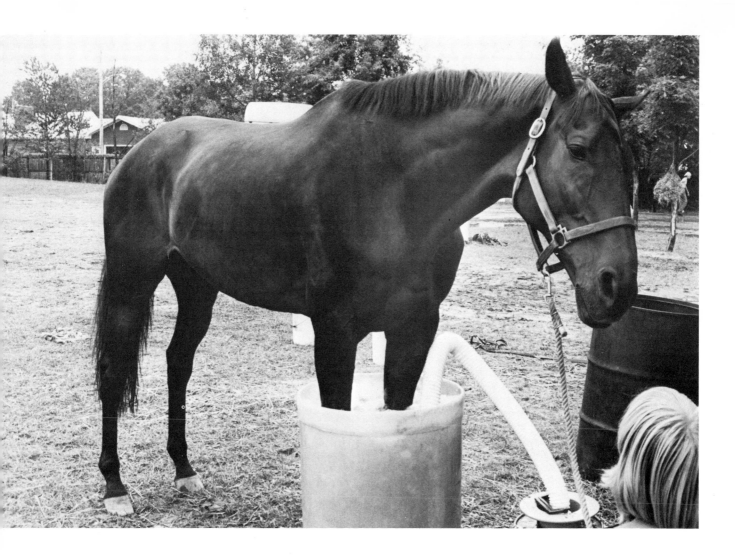

The groom walks the horse back and forth under the watchful eye of the trainer. Groom and trainer look carefully for any sign of lameness in the way the horse moves. They examine the horse's legs for soreness or swelling. If necessary, the trainer will order new horseshoes, treatment with ice water or liniment, special bandages, or an appointment with the vet.

If all is well, the groom walks the horse a few times around the stable area as a preliminary warmup before the day's training begins.

During the training, the horses are ridden by exercise riders. Most exercise riders don't work for one particular trainer, but go from stable to stable, often working five or more horses in a single morning. They must be expert riders, experienced at handling temperamental Thorough-breds in all kinds of situations. Many jockeys also work as exercise riders.

The exercise riders arrive with their own riding tack—saddle, saddlecloth, and the girth that straps the saddle to the horse's body. They report to the trainer for instructions.

The exercise rider straps on the tack and goes off to the racetrack or training track. The trainer may send a group of horses together, in order to observe several at once.

The kind of exercise ordered for a horse depends on the horse's condition and on the trainer's plans. It may be designed to prepare the horse for a specific race, or simply to maintain or increase speed and endurance. Horses in racing form are generally galloped lightly from one to two miles each day. A horse that is entered for a race will not be exercised at all that day.

About every two weeks, depending on the trainer, a horse is given a workout or blowout, a "race" at full speed over a predetermined distance, timed by the trainer. The blowout gives the horse a chance to extend itself, to stretch out between races. The horse's performance helps the trainer evaluate its condition and decide whether any changes should be made in its training.

While the horse is being exercised, the groom cleans out the stall. The feed tub and water bucket are removed and washed. Then, using a pitchfork, the groom takes out the wet or dirty straw and puts it into a large bucket, which is taken to a central dumping area. Fresh straw is put down. Finally the water bucket and hayrack are refilled and put in place.

A horse that is entered to run in a race might not even be taken out of the stall that day. The groom carefully mucks out the stall with the horse still inside, and removes the hayrack so the horse doesn't fill up on bulk. Small changes in the daily routine seem to let horses know when they're going to run. They get excited and a bit jittery in anticipation.

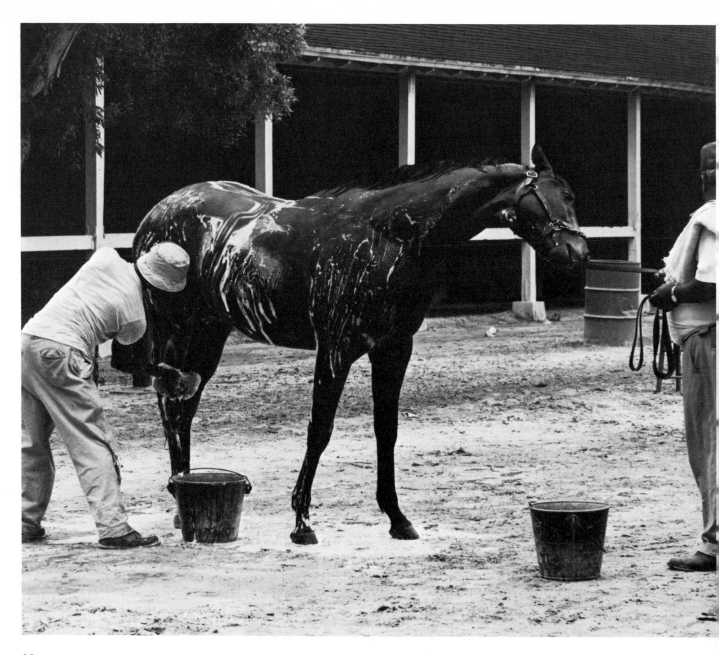

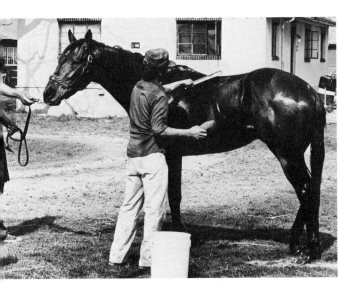

When the workout is finished, the exercise rider brings the horse back to the stable area, where the groom takes over. After walking the horse around to make sure no lameness has developed, the groom washes the horse down. An assistant holds the horse's halter, and the groom starts washing at the head and works back to the hindquarters, using a sponge and a pail of warm soapy water to which an antiseptic has been added. The horse is rinsed off, and excess water is removed with an aluminum scraper that looks like a long spoon. Finally the groom cleans and rinses the horse's hooves, which have accumulated dirt during the workout.

The horse's body is still heated from exercise and wet from being washed. Standing still, uncovered, the horse would cool off too fast and might get sick. So a stable hand called a hot walker cools the horse down slowly. A blanket is placed over the horse's back, and the hot walker walks the horse around, gradually folding back the blanket and stopping occasionally so the horse can drink, until the horse is completely dry. This takes about forty-five minutes. The horse is returned to the clean stall, where the protective bandages go back on.

By midmorning, almost all the stalls have been mucked out. The equipment is cleaned and laid out to dry, and the entire stable area is raked smooth and watered down. The stable hands take a break. The horses have finished their day's training, and they too can spend some time relaxing.

Relaxation is almost as important as exercise in a horse's conditioning. Nervous or fidgety horses waste a lot of energy that should be kept for racing, so trainers try to do whatever is needed to keep them calm. Some horses are given stablemates—goats, chickens, or cats; others seem to find the sound of a radio soothing.

Later in the morning the blacksmith may pay a visit. A horse in training must have new shoes at least once every four weeks. Racehorses wear special aluminum shoes, which are lightweight—important in racing—and much easier to work on than iron shoes. The blacksmith can bring all the necessary tools to the stable and shoe a horse's four hooves in about a half an hour.

First the old shoe is removed. A hoof that has grown too long will bother the horse, so the blacksmith trims off any excess. The preformed aluminum shoe is fitted, shaped on the portable anvil, and nailed on. Little felt pads are placed between the front hooves and the shoes, to help absorb the shock of running.

Shoeing is entirely painless to the horse.

The veterinarian makes barn calls too. Any horse that has a cold, a fever, or a leg ailment is examined and treated. If medication is prescribed, it is usually given by injection; it's hard to make horses swallow pills, but shots don't seem to bother them. The groom uses a device called a twitch, a stick with a loop of chain on the end, to keep the horse looking straight ahead. The loop is just tight enough to prevent the horse from turning to watch what the vet is doing. This makes the horse less likely to kick or rear up. Horses that are scheduled to race are given a checkup to make sure they are in top physical shape. The vet also advises the trainer if a change in diet or routine would improve a horse's condition.

At noon, the horses that will not be running are given a light lunch—some oats and grain, and fresh water. The horses that are to race just get water, no lunch. They will run better if they aren't carrying extra weight in the form of food or using part of their energy to digest it.

By 12:30 the racing fans are arriving at the track. The day's card—the list of the day's races—is printed in a program that can be bought on the way in. There are usually nine or ten races of varying distances. The names of the horses and jockeys, each horse's assigned weight (the weight the horse will be carrying) and post position number (the horse's position at the starting gate) are included in the program.

Near the grandstand is the paddock area, with an enclosure where the horses are saddled and a walking ring. As post time draws near, grooms bring the horses for the first race to the paddock area. They walk the horses around the ring for a while, giving them a chance to get used to the different surroundings and to relax. This is also the racing fans' first chance to look them over.

At the same time the jockeys who will ride in the first race are getting ready. Each jockey goes to the silks room to collect a shirt provided by the horse's owner. The colors of the "silks," which are actually made of rugged shiny nylon, designate the horse's owner or home stable. There are more than a thousand different color and pattern combinations in the silks room.

They dress in the jockeys' quarters, a large locker room with a big scale in the middle. A racetrack official, the clerk of scales, weighs each jockey—riding tack and all—before each race, to make sure the horse will be carrying its assigned weight, no more or less. Then the saddle, which belongs to the jockey, is taken to the paddock.

The groom brings the horse into the paddock. With the help of an assistant, the trainer carefully puts on the horse's saddlecloth, then the saddle, and straps the saddle on with an elastic girth. The horse gets another turn around the walking ring to get used to the feel of the saddle—which weighs only two or three pounds—and to relax further before the race.

Now the jockeys appear, dressed in the brightly colored silks and carrying long riding crops. They head for the center of the walking ring, where each jockey will meet with the horse's trainer to discuss strategy—the best way to race the horse on this particular day.

The paddock judge, the racetrack official in charge of activities in the paddock area, calls, "Get your riders up!" At this signal trainers and riders go to their horses, and the trainers give the jockeys a leg up on their mounts.

The groom leads the horse around the walking ring again, in full view of the spectators, giving rider and horse a chance to get used to each other.

The bugler sounds the traditional "call to post," letting people know that the horses are on their way to the racetrack.

Excited and eager to run, some high-strung horses may tire themselves out before the race begins. To keep them under control, outriders—people riding calm, easygoing horses—take hold of their bridles and guide them from the walking ring to the racing oval. Some well-behaved horses don't need outriders.

As the horses reach the racetrack, the bugler once again sounds the call to post. The horses seem to tiptoe onto the racing surface, which is softer than regular dirt. Over a base of tightly packed clay and sand is a three- to four-inch layer of loosely packed topsoil mixed with sand, which absorbs the initial impact of the horses' hooves as they run.

Still led by the outriders, the horses make one pass in front of the grandstand. This post parade gives the spectators a final chance to see the horses and riders before the race and try to pick the winner.

It is now just minutes till post time. The spectators rush to the betting windows to place bets on the horses of their choice, and the horses and outriders break into a jog, headed for the starting gate.

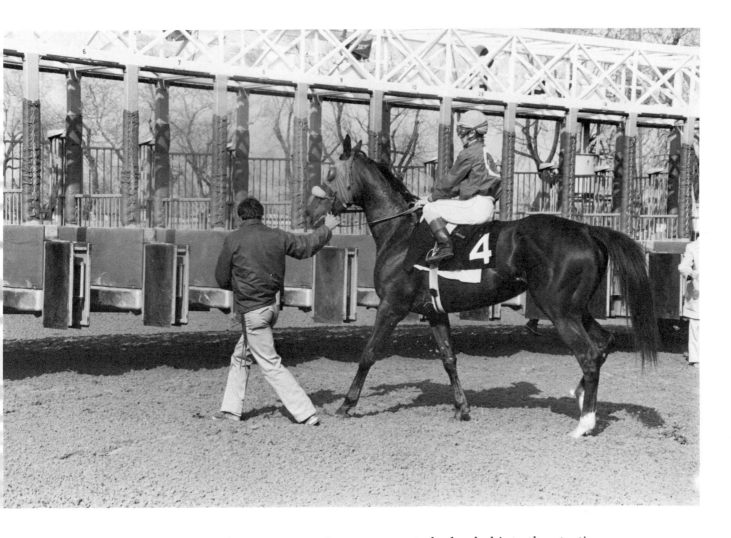

Each horse is turned over to an assistant starter to be loaded into the starting gate. The starting gate is a row of stalls, each just big enough to hold a horse and well padded for the horse's safety. Some horses resist being led into the narrow stalls; they may need to be blindfolded or backed in.

The assistant starter may squeeze into the stall with the horse and rider to make sure the horse is looking straight ahead, alert for the start of the race.

When the horses are all in line at the starting gate, the announcer tells the racing fans over the public address system, "It is now post time." The race will start at any moment.

The starter overlooks all the activity at the gate from a raised stand. A microphone connected to a speaker in the starting gate lets the starter communicate with the assistant starters and the jockeys.

After giving them a final warning that the race is about to begin, the starter presses the button that releases the gates. . . .

. . . and the gates fly open. "They're off!" says the announcer.

The announcer sits in a small glass-enclosed booth high atop the grandstand, directly overlooking the entire racetrack above the finish line. Before each race the announcer memorizes the names of all the horses entered and the colors of the racing silks, in order to identify the horses immediately during the race. Watching through high-powered binoculars, the announcer describes the race for the spectators, giving the position of each horse.

As they cross the finish line, the horses are moving so fast that they can't stop right away. The jockeys let up on the reins and stand up in their saddles, allowing their mounts to "run out" for about a quarter of a mile.

The winner is taken to the winner's circle, a small area on the racetrack where winner and crew are photographed. Then the groom takes the horse back to the stable.

The other horses are ridden back to their waiting grooms. The jockeys dismount, remove their tack, and weigh out. Then they go back to the jockeys' quarters to clean up, change, and wait for their next ride.

The grooms lead the horses back to the stable, where they are washed down, walked until they have cooled off, and put into their stalls for the night.

By early evening, another day's racing is finished, and the stands are empty.

Back at the stable the horses are given their dinner, the biggest meal of the day. It might include mash, cooked oats mixed with bran and molasses. Then the grooms remove the feed tubs, refill the water buckets, clean out any soiled straw from the stalls, rake the area around the stable, and go home.

And the night watchman settles down to begin his day at the races.

HAROLD ROTH was born in Austria and has lived in Montreal and in New York. His photographs have appeared in books, on calendars, and in numerous magazines in the United States and abroad. Mr. Roth's first book for Pantheon was *First Class! The Postal System in Action.* He lives in New York with his wife and their daughter, Alexis.

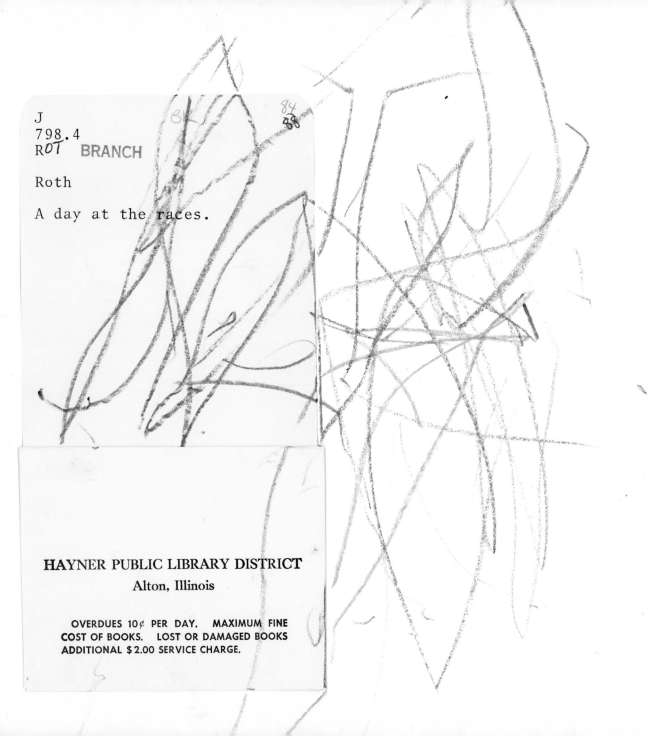

J
798.4
ROT **BRANCH**

Roth

A day at the races.